Butterfly VOYAGE

*B*ianca *B*owers

Butterfly VOYAGE

Copyright © 2018 by Bianca Bowers
Published by Paperfields Press

Book Cover Art © Anna Ismagilova, Shutterstock ID 129227303
Book Cover Design and Typesetting by Bianca Bowers
Interior Sketches © Bianca Bowers

All rights reserved. No part of this publication may be reproduced, distributed, or transmitted in any form or by any means, including photocopying, recording, or other electronic or mechanical methods, without the prior written permission of the publisher, except in the case of brief quotations embodied in critical reviews and certain other noncommercial uses permitted by copyright law. For permission requests, email the publisher: "Attention: Permissions" / info@paperfieldspress.com
www.paperfieldspress.com

A catalogue record for this book is available from the National Library of Australia

Printed and bound in Australia
ISBN-13: 978-0-6484426-0-8
eBook ISBN-13: 978-0-6484426-1-5

ENVIRONMENTAL RESPONSIBILITY
This book is printed using the print-on-demand-model i.e. it is only printed when an order has been received. This type of manufacturing reduces supply chain waste, greenhouse emissions, and conserves valuable natural resources.

Second edition
January 2020

For my daughter, son, and husband.

The Voyage

FOREWORD
PRELUDE   3
PART I
Spirit Message I, 30 May 2016   7
Sleeping, Like Beauty   10
Once Upon A Heart   12
Commandments   13
Pilgrim   14
Against the Odds   15
Like A Ghost   16
The Lost Girl   17
Smudges of Fear   18
A Girl Again   20
Extraction   21
Jagged Cruelty   22
Old Stories   23
Rosemary Flames   25
Woodland Ghosts   27
River   29

PART II
Spirit Message II, 12 August 2016   33
Birthday   34
Belief   35
Dreamscape   36
Wild Woman   37
White Horse   38
Map   39

The Raven Empress	40
Nightbird	42
Under Moonlight	44
Leda I - The Dragon and the Butterfly	46

PART III

Spirit Message III, 24 August 2016	55
Vampire Bride	57
Riverbed	58
Simmering	59
Excavate	60
Integrity	61
Mausoleum	63
Waiting	64
Bonsai	65
Bird's Eye View	66
Amongst The Bones	69
Skeleton Tree	70
Ghosts	71

PART IV

Spirit Message IV, 11 September 2016	75
Purple Oblivion	80
Rabbit Holes	81
The Flower of Life	82
Star	84
The Girl Who Saved The Moon	85
The Magic of Flowers	87
Whale Procession	89

Leda II - Wild Horses   91

PART V

Spirit Message V, 25 September 2016   97
Acorn   101
We Stand Still   102
Your Heart Is Not A War Machine   103
Revenge   104
Wake Up   105
Indigo Portal   107
The Jasmine Song Of Whales   109
Mystic   110
Spirit Message VI, 26 September 2016   111

PART VI

Spirit Message VII, 30 September 2016   115
Spirit Message VIII, 1 October 2016   117
Leda III - BEcome OR Become Extinct   119
Leda IV - A Spider's Nature   122
The Forest   125
Unicorn   126
Love is the Lotus   127
Paperweight   128
Incognito   129
Sea Dragon   131
Leda V - The Spider and the Python   133

PART VII

Spirit Message IX, 4 October 2016   139
Medicine Woman   143

Leda VI - The Nile Crocodiles	144
Woodland Death	148
April Fool	149
Distant Memory	150
Death Should Come But Once	151
The Art of Surrender	153
On The Verge	154
Burning Sun	155
Morphosis	157

PART VIII

Spirit Message X, 2 December 2016	161
Leftovers	164
Flower Of The Earth	165
Leda VII - Ceremonial Wings	166
The Cicada's Song	170
The Fates	172
Spirit Message XI, 1 September 2018	173
Spirit Message XII, 12 September 2018	176
BUTTERFLY VOYAGE ENDNOTES	178
ACKNOWLEDGEMENTS	181
ABOUT THE AUTHOR	183

Foreword

On 30 May, 2016, at 1.52 am, I woke from a dream and scribbled...

*I am the mother
who always loved you*

Seventy three lines later I had penned (or rather channelled) a cryptic poem that seemed to contain an urgent message. At that stage I had no idea what it meant, but my intuition told me that all would be revealed if I paid attention to the signs.

In the days that followed, lines from the poem started to materialise and more cryptic poems (or spirit messages as I now call them) were channelled.

Two weeks later, after a series of serendipitous events, I travelled out of state to attend a shamanic retreat where I took Ayahuasca for the first time. Ayahuasca is an entheogenic brew and spiritual medicine used by Shamans from the Amazon basin. It is said to clear spiritual baggage from current and previous lives.

The experience was both confronting and liberating, and ultimately sent me on a two year journey of deep self-reflection and healing.

Butterfly Voyage is a poetic account of that two year journey.

Prelude

Once upon a lifetime ago, you were born with a dragon's spirit and a butterfly's heart. Balance, was nature's intent.

Once upon a girl, you were nurtured with books and disciplined with bibles. You fell prey to hungry predators who tore your wings and left you for dead.

Once upon an adolescent, you swapped the flowers of courage, beauty, wonder and trust for the cave of survival. You turned your breath to fire, your words to arrows, and gave your butterfly heart to the dragon for safekeeping. The dragon, always your fierce protector, hid it in the deepest, darkest cavern of the earth's womb. When it returned, you, like Sleeping Beauty, had fallen into a deep sleep. And there you stayed, in that world of dreams and nightmares, until a familiar voice began to whisper…

I am the mother
who always loved you

Part i

"Hear the song within you
It calls you at night
while you dream
while you dream
And it means
Those wings
that look like ribs
are real
and the pain is not mistaken,
Butterfly"

Spirit Message I, 30 May, 2016 at 1.52 am

I am the mother
who always loved you

Feathers for arms
Tattoos for skin

I was the mother
She was the sin

Dreams forsake not
while I cradle your fall
between kingdoms

Ears for dragons
Call your name
you shall answer me
My child
Because I made you
I cradled you
I reared and revered you
Contemplate
I'm at the gate
I spiral and twist in the wind
like a desert chime
a charm
My child
The shock in your eyes, in your heart

It was me, not you,
Reminder, reminding
The bond between children
and their earth Madres

You will hear my whisper roar
through the trees
from now on
You will never forget
No longer slumber
The traffic is snail pace
You've won the race
in your heart and your head
You're not dead
You're not dead

My lips
are eyes
Lines in the sand
that snake like red

A willow
A cactus
A skull
A bed

You are sacred
You are sound

You be breeze / breathe
Breath and tails
Before your scales
Feet, foot
They step
They wait
But run now
Over desert sand
and sun
Rainbows
Fly
like birds

Hear the song within you
It calls you
at night
while you dream
while you dream
And it means
those wings
that look like ribs
are real;
the pain is not mistaken
Butterfly

I will call you back when it's time
In time
It is time

I'm a woman who's been
Sleeping, like Beauty
Life, passing like clouds
Questions, raging like storms
My Self, illusive as rainbows

Asleep

Paralysed

Amnesia

Oblivious to my royal veins
refusing thimbles, bloodletting on purpose

Waiting for a prince
Waiting for Godot
Until a twist
I never saw coming

My spirit mother
sent to wake me
by any means necessary
Dragons and butterflies
Fire and fables
Shape-shifting and ceremonies

Now, I'm a woman
stirring
A woman on a voyage
between kingdoms

Wrinkles of a life, ironing out
Wings, unhinged
Adventure, sprouting roots
The magic of Self, no disillusion.

Once Upon A Heart

LOVE
      f
      e
      L
      L

into a well of LOATHING

and
ever
since
then

it has been an

Ee
Cc
Hh
Oo

A Mother's call
growing louder at midnight

The dungeons are darkest
during winter

The truth is locked by
Commandments
that mean nothing today

I follow her words

                      like signposts, while I learn

to decipher their meaning

Like a

Pilgrim

I cross borders and oceans, follow the flight path of ravens
until my urban footprint is unrecognisable

From the lip of the crater
my signal reads SOS
A raven's feather

        p
   i
      v
          o
      t
  s

from the sky

I drive into a forest of crooked trunks
My notebook gets heavier

A heartbeat
A stirring

Rubber tyres on a dirt track
like quakes beneath my feet

Faded leaves
Blackened trunks

Everything has survived
Against the Odds
in this rocky soil

Evolution
Made stronger
angrier
defensive

Lost and lonely souls
parked
in the wilderness

But somehow
pink peyote[1] flowers
bloom
amongst nature's outcasts

When night falls
I Walk Like A Ghost
haunted
by the past

When my toes meet
the roots of the forest
I see a rusted cage
the trappings of survival

That was the night
I saw my ghost

The Lost Girl

dead and buried, I thought

with glassy eyes and dead flowers in her hair

A chilling message echoing from the cave of her soul

*"I couldn't stop you from killing the girl,
but I can stop you from killing the woman
you promised to be."*

On a blue window
I leave
Smudges of Fear

Three bars of heat
between my knees
and the Medicine man's feet

~

Ayahu[2] is inside
swallowed like semen

I hear chains rattle
see fingers point
at me
the marked woman
before her burning
before her ceremony
before her power runs out
before its renewed
before the virus mutates

I lose lashes
at the thought of this misfit
being burned at the stake

But it must be killed

Channel me
before I'm lost
Stamp like an animal
Shift the mountain

You warrior queen, you mother of life

Get out, I tell you, Get out
you liar of likeness
You've overstayed your welcome

I'm shutting off the power
taking away your bed
Tonight we go to war
I don't want you anymore

I will do this thing
this awful thing
to extract your poison from me

I want to run into the wood
naked
take trees for lovers
plunge roots into earth
rub skin against moss and bark
like a fairy awakening to magic in her wings

Instead, I am
A Girl Again
with burn marks on my wrist
They sting
like a lance searing flesh

Is this what I've done to myself?
A gentle spirit turned malevolent

I run into the woods
to escape the funeral in my head
and bargain with a raven
to swap places

I cling to the roots of self
I should be striving to dispossess
Fight the storm and simultaneously bend with it

deep inside me
trauma aches like sensitive teeth

Extraction
is a solution I am at odds with
At what cost do I remove this pain?
Do I want to remove this pain?
So familiar it has become
so integral it is
What will grow in its place
if anything?

There are demons in my head
but I am only now
seeing their faces on the page

My own words, reserved for self,
staring back with
seasoned hatred, with

Jagged Cruelty

They say things
I wouldn't utter
to enemies

So, why then
is it acceptable to treat
ME
this way?

An invasion of

Old Stories

is upon you
The stories you gathered like tinder
and lit to burn yourself

Forgive yourself
be a warrior
Remind yourself
about the pain that brought you here

The beginning
is where the answer
to every question
lives
Genesis—
that is the truth to unlock
and unhinge this impasse

Go back
Right now
Don't falter, don't wait
Don't tell yourself those stories
those lies you think are truth

They are not
They are not

They are century-old stories
Collected and hard wired
Cross circuited to short circuit

It's the stories that kill
So kill the stories
and save love

I trust her advice
by now
Pen the beginnings
of a crimson paper trail
shorthand and long
I bleed easier through ink
the bottomless well of a subterranean heart

Outside
my breath turns to smoke
as I sacrifice each syllable to

Rosemary Flames

I watch the embers dance
up
into the atmosphere
Visceral confessions
purged by fire

Witness them space travel
No longer captive
within my

Sahasrara[3]
Ajna
Vishuddha
Anahata
Manipura

Svadhishthana
Muladhara

When fire returns to the sky
I will know freedom

It's dark
All I can see is the skeletons of trees
Tall, stark, porcelain limbs

Woodland Ghosts

that I'm not afraid of

Rain spits
I feel it against exposed skin
Nose, cheeks, lashes

Tree tops seem to reach
the sky

I am there
where darkness meets the ground
like a bonfire waiting to ignite

Their naked limbs remind me
of something
about myself

I search for what it is
Hear them whisper
to me

They are my guardians
We are lone sentinels

who have died together
Burned together
between kingdoms
across centuries

Like vampires
we remember the pain
but we no longer bleed

Like a

River

water will flow
regardless of resistance

Big changes have occurred

Each day
the resistance to change
will cause white water in the river
of self-doubt

Each day
the futility of resistance
will smooth the boulders
of fear

Each day
the truth of change
will reveal itself a little more

until
there is no question

Part ii

"I can see your wings
Can you?
Paint them on if you must
but fly you will"

Spirit Message II, 12 August 2016 at 11 pm

Butterfly
I'm awake while you dream

Let your arms
fall off
like tree limbs
in a storm
Old and worn

Trees are thicker
than alpine forests
Lakes have frozen over
You can walk on water now

The desert
waits and shifts
Underfoot
camels are thirsty
tents are pitched
The night is a blanket of stars
for us to count

I can see your wings
Can you?
Paint them on if you must
But fly you will

Today is your

Birthday

Proof that magic exists
in your human world

Follow me, old friend
I know a peaceful place
beneath the forest's skin
where magic crackles like stars
and waxes in sync with Mother Moon

A place where ancestors forgive
and karma forgets

You always were a totem to me
A native spirit beneath your war paint

Belief
is modern magic
It's music and mayhem
a collision of intention
a picnic between heart and head
Don't deny yourself the possibility of impossibilities
because they wait for you
if you really want them

Mountainous clouds
usher me into the forest
where winter pitches her tent
where time is never spent
where oxygen has roots

There are days when I never want to sleep
and hours when I can think of nothing else

My
Dreamscape
calls me
like scorched grass calls the rain

I am in the forest
at first light
closer to myself than ever before

The mountain is a
Wild Woman
who knows my name
Her blue breath hovers
like a cloud
She whispers no more
Sings about dragons
and whales
on a voyage beside me

Between the trees
I travel
in search of nests that cradle
the bones of my temple

I see a curve in my reality
a skewing of fate
a fissure in the sky
Feel the reverberation
of my own ripple
and understand I must follow

I dream of a

White Horse

It calls me to explore
spiritual realms and dimensions
        through meditation, vision quests and shamanic journeying
before it fades to black
and I am underground—
                a Victorian woman
                with heels and hat—

I follow the voice
of a little girl
to a room lit with fireflies
On tiptoes she carefully lifts
a bird cage off a row of shelves
presses it into my chest
Behind the bars, a raven
with thick wings
and emerald eyes nudges my ribs with her beak and says:

        "I have much to teach you
                about the language of freedom."

The ravens follow me again
or is it I who follow them?
Dark messengers of light
Wisdom so instinctual
it already dwells
inside my bones
beneath my skin

I follow a trail of black feathers
until I find a
Map
buried beneath a rock

Pines grow thicker here
Roots dig deeper
Traffic thins

I wade into a sea of green needles
to find her
The Raven Empress
who reigns over another dimension

where the air ripples
if you dare touch it
if you dare enter

A parallel kingdom where your soul resides
the kingdom you search for every mortal day
the kingdom your soul visits in dreams

That parallel kingdom shimmers here;
I have found it
while lucid
after decades of incarnations
of voyages, mazes, puzzles, exile

The green haze heals like a lover's embrace
a deep welcome I've never known

Now that I've found it

I shall not straddle that mortal cell
another day

I am conversing
in the language of freedom
Liberty becomes me
I will forfeit no jewel of myself
again

Black lashes and green eyes
lead me into the forest
A sacrifice has been made
the ribcage of my past
picked bare by corvids
A ritual of trees awaits
branches I must climb
new heights to scale

I slip into a black cloak
cold against my skin
I am the raven queen
hours before her crown is bestowed
Beak and wings
a night sky filled with feathers

The night breathes its cold breath
on the nape of my neck
I shiver
There is magic inside me
It crackles and sparks

I am not human
not witch, I am a

Night Bird
a winged messenger
who flies between kingdoms

A time traveller

who can lead you to that bridge
where your body meets your soul
where authenticity fleshes out the bones of your
identity

Follow me
when dusk orients itself
when night transmutes
into soul

Follow me
don't wait
there is life to be tasted and kissed
bathed and powdered

A rosemary forest
thick with scent
I go deeper
to find what is lost

Jasmine flowers beside a camp fire
Hoop pines shape shift
Under Moonlight
like a human during the day

The forest closes in
a canopy of terrestrial stars
Shadows are visible
when dusk pirouettes

I pull night around my shoulders
like a shawl
Balance;
embrace and isolation
in a teaspoon

There are stars in the ocean
tonight
a twisty spine
symmetrical lovers
adrift

                Night clouds drift like smoke signals
                  Dark is a ceremony unto itself
                          exposed
                          revealed

                                          I call her mother

She calls me daughter

                I step into her palm
              when morning yawns
        Back into the belly of the world
                she delivers me
              where I don't belong
                With a reminder
          that voyages are a slow
              unfolding of wings

Leda i

The Dragon And The Butterfly

I crawled through a hedge, abloom with star jasmine, and came face to face with a black dragon. Its purple breast evoked the dragon in Sleeping Beauty—my favourite childhood story.

It rose into the air, when I stepped toward it, and breathed its fiery breath towards the clouds.

I raised my hand like a white flag and said, "I'm not afraid. Please, will you stay."

It hovered for a while, as if to be sure, then descended to the ground, sunk its claws into the fresh cut grass, and stood opposite me. I lifted my chin to meet its eyes, and it bowed its head to meet mine. Green and blue eyes interlocked. The overwhelming sense of déjà vu. A dream, perhaps, though it had the hallmarks of a memory.

"Climb onto my back," it said lowering and flattening itself on the grass.

"How do I get on without hurting you?" I said.

"You won't hurt me," it said. "Step onto my tail and walk the length of my back until you reach my neck. Then sit down, and wrap your arms and legs around me."

I complied without hesitation and whispered, "ready", once I'd shimmed into position. Its powerful black wings arched over my head like an angel's halo and we ascended into the sun-studded sky within seconds.

I watched in wonder as we flew through wisps of clouds, across verdant valleys and over blue mountains. I closed my eyes and laid my cheek against its neck. Its purple scales were as warm as human skin. I wondered if the dragon had a name.

Before I could voice the question out loud, it spoke.

"Leda," she said.

"How did you know?"

'Telepathy," she said. "Just like you."

"Is that what it is?" I said.

"You've always had the gift, but you guard it like a shameful secret."

"I wasn't sure," I said, "and it's not something I can admit in my world."

"I know," she said. "There is so much your human world is incapable of comprehending."

"Leda is a beautiful name," I said. "What does it mean?"

"It means woman. The name was bestowed on me by an ancient dragon queen with breath of fire and words that could wound and heal. The queen's name was Blue. Like the ocean and sky, but she existed long before both."

"You remind me of the dragon in Sleeping Beauty," I said. "Not in a bad way. I never considered the dragon to be bad."

"The gatekeepers and truth twisters in your human world have abused and misappropriated so much," she said. "The colour black has been used to depict evil and dark magic, but that is simply not true. Black also possesses the power of absorption — be that positive or negative energy — which is probably one of the reasons why it's been associated with negativity over the centuries."

Leda's wings smoothed out as we approached a purple horizon, and she dipped her head to descend. My stomach dropped ever so briefly before we landed in a field with a gentle tap. The air was alive with the mist of a thousand blue and violet butterflies weaving in and out of tall lavender stalks.

"Is it safe for a dragon and a human to tread in such a delicate and fragile place?" I said.

"Funny you should say that," she said, "because it's the reason I brought you here."

I followed behind her, watching her clawed-feet pad as softly as a kitten's paws through the lavender field. The butterflies didn't seem to mind. They wafted in and out of the purple flowers, alighting on Leda's wing tips and occasionally on the spike above her nostrils. The scene was serene. Both seemed to be aware and respectful of the other. Leda stopped walking and turned to face me.

"What you see here," she said, "is balance."

"Balance," I repeated and nodded.

"Yes," she said. "Balance is the key to everything. It is nature's way. When there is imbalance, trouble arises and nature works against itself."

"Tell me more," I said.

"You possess the heart of a delicate butterfly, but you hide it beneath your black dragon armour."

"I'm sorry," I said, "I am always on the defensive."

"You don't need to apologise," she said. "But you need to know that breathing fire and posturing in defence will only result in isolation and wearing yourself out."

I nodded my understanding.

"I've brought you here to show you that there is no need for the butterfly and dragon to be in conflict. It is possible for them to co-exist, so long as there is balance."

"I understand," I said, "but it's easier said than done."

"First, the lesson," she said, "then the learning, as many times as it takes, until we finally reach the knowing." She nudged me with her nose and I felt love stirring from a place of unfathomable depth.

    We sat together in that lavender field, for what seemed like months, watching the butterflies waft and flutter in and amongst the flowers like peaceful little clouds. I thought about what Leda had said. Butterflies were delicate and unprotected in a predatory environment. Still, they ventured out in search of beautiful flowers. They didn't hide away in fear.

    I thought about my own behaviour. I had spent my life withdrawing, hiding and arming myself because I'd been hurt out in the world more times than I cared to admit. After many bad experiences I decided that everybody was the enemy and treated them accordingly. But Leda was right. My behaviour had not hurt my enemy. It had only hurt me. I had the strength and ferocity of the dragon to protect me, but I had to learn to balance that armour with vulnerability. For the sake of my heart. For the sake of my overall wellbeing.

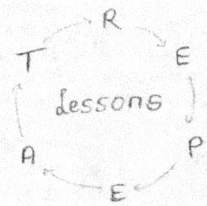

Part iii

"Cocoons dissolve eventually
like moth wings
like night
like day
Everything fades to ash
my friend"

Spirit Message III, 24 August 2016 at 10pm

Hold the jade[4] stone tonight
Dreams will come
on wings
winged dreams will visit
winged visitors will dream
Night suffused with jasmine
will soar
toward a fragrant moon
of glass and sheet

Torture not yourself
my child
Your mouth can penetrate
perpetrate lies
Still, hold on
Cocoons dissolve eventually
like moth wings
like night
like day
Everything fades to ash
my friend

Give yourself wings
They are yours to take
yours for the taking
So take them
Why do you wait?
Hesitate?

Wait to hesitate, hesitate to wait
Instead, go
I have opened the door
to love
It is yours, my love
Love is yours

You special one
You loved one
Beloved
Hear that word, in all its forms
Love
It is yours
Love is yours
My love, you are loved, love yourself
For god's sake
Love yourself
Don't apologise
Be irreverent
Be yourself
That's all there is

You deserve it all. Go, look in the mirror and say, "I deserve it all."

Do it now.
That's it.
Now, it is done. It is done.

There is a ghost who lives inside me

Vampire Bride

Corpse, in a tattered dress
I don't know where she came from
or what she wants
but every time the full moon glows
she rises from my chest
and hovers above my ribcage
as if I am her home

She is deathly pale
just like a corpse should be,
I guess
Untouched by the sun (like me and my freckles)

I'm unsure why
but I love her
She means me no harm
and there are worse things to be
than a cemetery

I dream from the

Riverbed

watch pines sway
along the falls

A stone totem
is where I'm buried
like doubt

But I don't cry

Currents fight my ambition
attempt to drag my bones
to safety
but darkness is heavier
than water
So, I stay a while—
feel the weight of love underwater
sink into the depths of my own heart
instead of swim.

A raven carries winter in its beak
while youth gallops around me

I can make believe
touch the sky without heels
but pretending
is certain death
a
Simmering
of self
that refuses to catalyse

I visit the cemetery to

Excavate

remnants of self-love

Scabs of fallen branches
beneath my feet
I follow a trail
of trinkets brought by humans
Afterlife gifts to salve terrestrial fears
Childhood beliefs, bedrock
in adult brains

The tip of a lesson
points right at me
with its mossy eyes
and calloused fingers

I'm looking for peace without the body count
yet I've been armed for so long
Surrender
has such a perilous ring
to it

Wind whirs like traffic
between graves and trees
Skinks chase the sun
between blades abuzz
with cicadas

There are children here
in the ruins, in the wreckage
They feed nature with their hope
Their laughter echoes in the wind

We think we're unwelcome
but they tell me otherwise
Their love for life has not changed
it is our view of death that needs fixing

If this is all we are
a number on an arrow
in a garden littered with bones
Then it is life-and-death to follow
an authentic path, to
treat ourselves with

Integrity

If life is a story
with birth, the beginning
death, the end

what is the nature of our living?

Are we
designing
or creating
or controlling
or dying, piecemeal...

My footsteps echo
in the marble

Mausoleum

A reminder of the
                        well,
                    where
                my heart
          used to live and love

An echo that reverberates differently
while my house undergoes a change
in acoustics
But still attempts to coax me

back into hiding
one day at a time

I fight withdrawal
Will not surrender
to that comfortable
darkness anymore

My ego hides in the tall grass;
A hungry wolf in the dry season.

I feel its deception
Brush against my cheek
See its reflection shimmer
in the overhead clouds
And I know this
Waiting
is worthwhile

There is a dreaming tree
within me

copper leaves and turquoise blooms
spidery roots for veins

buried in an earth womb
a foetus stunted
by the drought of doubt

a Bonsai
immaculately restrained

She sends violet lightning
to electrify hardwires
and summons rainy
tears

We watch and wait
for seeds to grow

On the ridge, I have a

Bird's Eye View

Raven's caw
draws my attention to the crater
where life and death converge
where thickened trunks bulge with wisdom
where weathered tombstones are stacked with history
where crows use their beaks to click an ancient morse code
where buried bones fertilise earth
in an indomitable cycle

This place that draws me
magnetic
is full of souls, but empty of people
and this small distinction clarifies why
I'm at home here
amidst the wreckage
because my vision is elsewhere
and this is not wreckage
It's a peaceful exchange between silence and
mindfulness,
an unconditional acceptance
off limits to the living
    who remember to forget
    who fill silences with shallow graves
    who empty words of meaning
    who live to hide

This human interference
that wears me down
and anchors my doubt
is absent here - dead
and the death of meaningless emptiness is, for me, life giving
Breath and blood and heartbeat
All that I strive and struggle for
against the flow of human traffic
the wreckage of the living

I am part of a circle, a cycle
one without limitation, if I choose
to break and forge another

This is my power
our power
We choose everyday

For this life is not about the killing
of self and others
but the continued transformation, evolution,
metamorphosis of all

For we must know
that whatever we destroy
will trigger a self-destruction

And how do we know we've gone too far?
I'll tell you. While I sit here, amongst the tombs,

and I see more life, more harmony
more peace
more creation
more renewal here
than I do in that kingdom of skyscrapers
in the distance
in the back to back coffins
of the suburbs

It is nature. We are nature
We are natural, but have turned
unnatural. Imbalanced. Working against our soul's DNA.

WE are ghosts
held hostage by machines
lest we Rise from concrete
Scratch the itch of our wings
and learn to fly

Now is upon us
Tomorrow happened yesterday
Today is all we have left.

I hear Raven's song
Her sonnet of love
to this earth, our mother

Age-old wisdom
tucked betwixt her feathers
Emerald eyes that seek out portals
A beak that penetrates netherworld dimensions

She has walked
Amongst the Bones
and seen the circle

I dream at the trunk of a

Skeleton Tree

Ravens congregate along its bony limbs

If I'd known
shadows were distorted trunks
in dappled sunlight
I'd have scarred the monster
and bled less

The sky is emptied of cloudy pedestrians
but words fall like rain
into the reservoir of my journal

I wake to find my old skin
is loose as a summer dress

Ghosts

rise from my chest
their haunting no longer a threat

I watch their torn robes
flutter
in the oncoming breeze
The mast of a new shipwreck
raises its hand in distress

The space they filled

echoes
like falling water

but the trees have taken root
and a rainforest is possible
in time

Part iv

*"Sleep comes
but don't wait for rabbits
to fetch you, to call you
Follow your own guide
down those magical holes
that only you can see"*

Spirit Message IV, 11 September 2016 at 8.54pm

A blue empress butterfly
wafts into the sheet of night
that is darkness and spirit world
combined

Shape shifting is nigh
Sigh, sigh, yawn and sigh
Nocturnal teacups wait for your lips
to sip
Sleep comes, but don't wait for rabbits
to fetch you, to call you
Follow your own guide down those magical holes
that only you can see
In the dark, in the light, when it's dark and out of sight

Twinkle moons and celestine stars
from Egypt, Nile crocodiles
in shallow depths to navigate and
pull you through mires and moors
that sail and swish in windy willows
Where crabs scurry amidst buried bones of sailors, of men,
of glorious bastards who never took no for an answer—
not when rebuked nor revoked
They poked their tongues at authority—
the bats[5] with batons
who fly in the face of reason
They are not soldiers, there is no fortune
Failing and flailing and falling

Yes, you see it
These words you love and worship
are so unreliable at times

Peeling paint and ceiling of sistine
cannot benefit art or
painters who return to God for no reason
because of treason
They surrender their arms — their creative arms
to a sky full of wimps and beards[6]
who cannot see reason, nor speak against treason
for they are the kings of unruly rubbish
They have slowed progress with their dope
and hogwash[7]

The birds know better
Always have. Always will.
Follow their beaks, their wings
Seek solace in their feathers and their eyes of emerald green, My
Raven queen, my shape shifting queen
who moved through sand, shifted the desert with her thoughts
and stepped on toes to win the hearts of the chosen kingdom[8]
that will rise in glory once more
When she remembers[9] her place, her power, her memory, her
position in this chess game of life that persists beyond the curtain
of sails that travail the seven seas
Like explorers of old, battered old souls that fought to find out
what lay behind the gates of gold and silver
Of copper lips and ragtime eyes
Of showdowns and horsemen

Of guns and slingers
Of glory and glorious and glory-be-wannabes
Gold, my love, my queen of antiquity
Gold is what you are, is where you are
Is what you'll be, is where you'll be

Rise into your crown
Seek the glory that is yours
By birthright
By rights be birthed
Sing, sing, sing your song
that waits to be discovered deep within the walls of your chest
You songbird of Galilee[10]
where trials and tribulations are nothing more than
empty pots

Be gone now, my daughter, to your place of birth
that birthplace of trees and forests
that shelter your eyes from prying eyes who die in the shade of
your power
Let them go, meaningless rubies in an emerald forest
Creeks that meander and drift to places not on the map
not of this world, You understand
my tongue is so foreign, but you understand it all

I plead, don't bleed anymore
for chaps and chops that stink of yesterday's dogma
The bones of broken promises will choke you
That's no joke, you know
It's time to move on, move forward, move away from the

flame that burns, the fire that seethes.
Move, don't melt
Move, before you melt
Move, I said move
Yes, I meant move
Move
Move
Move
Move
Movements
Moving
Moving
There is more than one meaning for words, for things, for people, for life

Direction is a curse
Follow your heart like a horse follows the wind
Stop asking and smell flowers on the path
Count colours as you wade into the ocean
Spill your heart like ink
Let it out, let it go, let it sink into the page
be not afraid of love
nor loving

Own your self
Own your heart

Close the curtains for the last time on that self that shifts like a snake
Open the blind to a new sun that shines always
even for the moon who steals its light at night

And now we're back to the beginning
to that century old tale of woe is me
My woe is me
But it doesn't have to be
if you choose to leave it
in yesterday's quicksand

It's time to sleep and dream
to dream while you sleep
to work your shadows into light
The work that happens after dark
is deep
Healing
is buried deep
Whale will show you the way
when you follow its tail/tale
of diving and migrating
of singing and chanting
of sighing and denying no more
Sleep well and sleep long
Goodnight

I see her sometimes
between decaying buildings
in the eyes of ravens
Illusive, yet present
I want to chase her down
and leave her be
Bewitching, bohemian
marching to war with her words, like me
only she knows more than I do
in this life, at least,
I close my eyes
wait for that

Purple Oblivion
where our spirits rendezvous

I wander the forest by day
for there is perspicuity amongst Junipers

But the truth about daylight
is that sky of reality
and subliminal incentive to count
clouds of impossibilities

No

I prefer the night
When stars outnumber clouds
When the moon commands the sky
like a high priestess
When my head is forced, much like my eyes,
to search deeper, to find

Rabbit Holes

- real and imaginary -

For the answers to impossible clouds
do not exist in the Sun's domain
Only the Moon's
For the Moon is Mother of
Intuition
and only she can see
the Butterfly
beyond the Chrysalis

I am barefoot in the temple of music
rice grains, confetti, scattered
in a circle
The Flower of Life
in my hand

I follow a whisper
She has called me before
when I was submerged
when my lungs were waterlogged
But I am above ground again
My diaphanous wings recharged
after many days in the sun
and nights under moonlight

My skin is new
primed for graffiti
a map of me
to never forget
again
who I am
and what I've become

The wind carries her voice
like a bird on the wing
and I follow without fear
for she has saved me already

There is light in her eyes
and wisdom on her tongue

She is the mother of my empowerment
the spine of my authenticity
the source of my creativity

The butterfly hatched
The dragon unleashed

She gave me the

Star

I had wished upon as a girl
in pink ballet shoes

    "Why is it so much bigger than the others?" I said.
    "It is a star who never gave up on its dream," she said.

She talked of thieves
who had come and gone over the years
Attempts to abduct
the baby star from darkened skies
But Mother Moon, a fierce protector,
who knew of a destiny beyond stratosphere,
had intervened

    "With this star comes great responsibility," she said. "Are you ready for what comes next?"

    I opened my mouth to answer.

    "Hush," she said. "You needn't answer. Just prepare yourself
for a cosmic curtain call."

I saved the moon from drowning when I was a child. On an upside down day—a lit sky without a sun, a pine lake glowing like a night light— I waded waist-deep to discover the moon beneath the surface. Neither floating nor sinking, but mysteriously submerged.

When I touched it, it glowed, then whimpered.
"Leda says that love can heal" I said, scooping it into my palms.
"It's true," she said, gasping for air, "love can heal everything".

She nudged my hands enough to break free, then floated up into the sky. Up and up and up, she drifted, until my head was tilted right back and she was a crown in the sky once again. I stood and watched in awe until daylight dissolved into twilight.

When I heard my mother's voice calling me inside for dinner, I hesitated, but only for a split second, because a shooting star rose and travelled across the moon. I watched it until it dropped, then fell at my feet. It sparked and hissed and fizzled, leaving nothing but a rock, with a note that said:

Thank you, sweet child. I will never forget your heart. But, a day might come when you forget...

A day when you feel limited. A day when you doubt yourself and your dreams. A day when you can summon nothing but tears. And whenever you have those days, take this note out and remind yourself that

YOU ARE

The Girl Who Saved the Moon

xoxo

I asked

The Magic of flowers

to grant one wish

Because I had heard whisperings —
      beneath the weeping willow
      one lonely, hot summer —
that flower magic was the purest
and most discerning

Flower magic knew what a woman yearned for
secretly
in the deepest recesses of her literary heart

Flower magic knew
that no woman could speak of
               her secret desire
for consequences were oft disastrous
and no woman wanted to destroy
when it was her birthright to create

I waited
      for the sky to close its eyes
      and sleep
before I followed the moonlit shadows
along the riverbank
to where the weeping willow bowed its head
toward the water

(unlike the other trees who reached skyward
as if it too was an anomaly
that desired something different)

I kneeled at the base of the trunk
found a rock as smooth as human skin...
A single touch is all I needed to unleash the magical blooms
                As white as magnolias
                As delicate as hyacinth
                As fragrant as wisteria

With open eyes and heart
exposed
I surrendered to magic
and blew those flowers
                like Dandelions
                Designed to travel far
                Destined to reach their destination.

Whale Procession

I drowned in squid ink
landed on the ocean floor
Clouds of sand engulfed me
like a great white's jaws
An army of jellyfish
passed overhead —
a beautiful funeral procession

Once death settled
my essence hovered — a reluctant apparition
I felt the starfish twitch beneath me
Spied sea dragons rocking to and fro
in the current

A school of parrot fish swam past
and a sea urchin opened its door

Then, Silence
as long as a pier.

That hovering essence transmuted
effervescent
A tiny whirlpool
above my chest
primed for the ocean to siphon

And then, the sound of whales

calling and wailing
singing their oceanic lullaby
So haunting and comforting
at once

They arrived in triangle formation
Mama at the front, pups behind her

My back arched as she scooped me up
into her world
My swirling essence, she blew
from her blowhole

And I,
I became cargo
To be transported, perhaps
to my next adventure

Leda ii

Wild Horses

Leda flew me away from the valley of butterflies, over mountains, and toward an open range where wild horses ran in the direction of the wind. We landed on a mountain peak and watched them run as the sun rose like a heart rising above the valley.

"Wild horses are not like sheep," said Leda. "Sheep are guided by fear. They follow the one in front, and do not think independently."

"With the exception of the black sheep," I said.

"There's that term 'black' again," she said. "That which society has dubbed negative, when they really mean too powerful."

"I have felt like a black sheep my whole life," I said.

Leda rubbed her wing against my shoulder and said, "Instead of seeing it as a negative, see it for what it is — unique, powerful and rare. The black sheep possesses the ability to see the Judas among the flock and turn the other sheep. But their fear is usually too great, and their comfort with discomfort keeps them trapped and stops them from progressing."

"I know that's not a bad thing, but it doesn't make for a smooth and easy life," I said.

"Black is your power," said Leda. "Don't give people permission to sideline or malign your otherness as they have done in the past. Recognise that you are unique and embrace it."

"Again, I know this conceptually, but I find it challenging (to put it mildly) to value myself and my gifts in a world that values the superficial."

"Let's get back to the horses for a minute," she said. "What do you think the difference is between these wild horses and sheep, or even wild horses and domesticated horses?"

I studied them for a minute before I spoke. "The obvious difference is freedom and enslavement" I said.

"That is the main difference, but there is more," she said. "These wild horses are one hundred percent in tune with their instincts. Wild horses have not been enslaved by conditioning and fear. They roam free, just as nature intended. Wild horses love to run (in tune with their natural instincts), but domesticated horses are trained to run and stop on command. Humans have turned the horse's natural instinct against itself."

"Humans have excelled in that department," I said.

"People, unlike sheep and horses, have a choice," said Leda, "but people have chosen fear over instinct."

"Choose love over fear," I said. "This is my ultimate lesson?"

"Trust your instincts and champion what makes you unique," said Leda. "Those are the lessons, Butterfly."

Part v

"Wisdom lies in coffins now
below ground zero
Hearts will rise
to disguise the skies
from bombs and planes
trains and guns
that shoot to kill
and kill the youth
for no other reason than revenge"

Spirit Message v, 25 September 2016 at 9.41pm

A fish moon forgets
to swim against the tide of life
that swills and swirls and sinks, like an anchored hook

Leavened bread to feed the 5000
Fish loaves for the hungry,
for those who didn't believe, or couldn't believe, or lacked faith
Oh Ye of little faith…
I haven't left
I'm always here
We are bound, we are bonded
Bountiful with bounty we will be

Let it go, let it all go
Free yourself you must
You've started, don't lambast yourself
It all takes time, even this, even you, even us
It takes time
Be patient
Sleep comes slowly
to sift your dreams, clean and pure
The mud is gargled eventually
Battle not with words and wisdom
It all comes when it's ready
Rest up, while it's travelling
nothing is lost
It simply means that bigger and
better is hurtling toward you

Hustle and bustle
No time to whistle
This is where you've come from, but it's not where you're going
Peace and tranquility is where it's at
Peace and tranquility you'll wear like a hat
Magic and mystery
Foxes and bears
will return to teach

Wisdom lies in coffins now
below ground zero
Hearts will rise to disguise the skies
from bombs and planes and trains and guns
that shoot to kill, and kill the youth for no other reason than
revenge of hapless selves who don't know a damn thing
Hapless and hopeless and heartless

There I go, with my words a marching
to war
Oh well, that's my spell, my words, like yours are daggers and
bones and beasts and blues and blossoms that bloom like fish
schools under the sea
Fish on my mind, so blue and moonlike
Or moonlight
They bloom
They bloom
Below the moon

Look beyond the sill
into the garden of dreams
where you rake up leaves that haven't fallen

What does that mean?
It means that doubt is a spark that lifts its voice when conjured
So don't conjure doubt
Free your mind
of demands and constraints
before you faint
Let go and let Glory
Glory is the feminine of god, not goddess.
Goddess is its own thing
Its own beautiful thing that cannot be sold as anything else

Listen while I speak
between riddles
I'm there, I'm everywhere
Pay attention to clues
The voice, the advice, the images, the messages
They're all coming for a reason
Don't discount a single one
Intuition is the answer
to burnt offerings
So make a pledge to listen to that voice
You know what it said
Don't waste your tongue on explanations
It matters not what others plot
You have the answers deep inside

Like spring seeds that suddenly sprout
Let go of doubt
Let go of sin
Sin is a swear word that should be banned
It's rubbish, it's rude, it's thoroughly crude

Headache material from centuries old
told and sold
bought and bitten
Nonsense and no sense
But this you know
You cracked that egg a long time ago

Tonight you will go far and away
Far and wide
To the skies
To disguise
To wisen (wizen) your whims
A jewel, a crown
Rise into your crown
You will, you will

Goodnight
Goodnight
while you travel away from yourself
to find yourself, out in the ether
Bones and skin
Wings and Wands
They wait for you
like wizard's food
Goodnight, go dream

She rises from the earth
like morning mist
like summer blades

She spreads her arms like wedge tail wings
Her love, she spreads like roots
Offers branches to all
who seek her shade
Even the buzzards who could do better
but know no different

Your heart is not an
Acorn
forever
Let it grow into an oak

The fish swim in circles and

We Stand Still

What is this madness that churns the waters red?
Spent and sold in a cage
While we cry, "untie our hands, set us free."
But there is more than one escape route...
If, we choose to listen,
to messengers, who rouse inner truths
If, we risk free fall,
from the trapdoor of illusion

Abandonment can mean many things
when the mind is free

Crescent moons collide with cathedrals
From the rooftop I hear chanting and prayer
Energy flows like ribbons of colour
Doves gather with thunderous wings
We cannot think about change anymore
We Must Act
We've been comfortable too long
the edge roars for our attention
Footsteps echo
armies march to war
Your hands can aim a gun
but not your heart, even when it's broke, suffering

Your Heart Is Not A War Machine

Slide not toward destruction
even though it is easier than loving
even though fear is paralysing
You are stronger than you think
You are greater than your weaknesses
You are more beautiful than your reflection
Embrace what is,
I beg you.

I press my cheek against turquoise
Izniks
A Mediterranean Refuge
after a thousand days in the desert

The world outside succumbs
to the moon watch

The beliefs of ancestors haunt
alleyways and heads of men
Women shroud their hearts in silk

The wild truth keeps growing in
the garden, like weeds
Cannot kill it with silence
or blood-stained regret

Revenge
as hot as the sun
to scorch a field of wilting flowers
is one thing, but to disdain the rain
and burn the whole forest
is madness in any century.

This earth glows;
a crescent within the super universe

Mother Nature
She is vibrant
Don't kill her with your dullness
Sharpen your senses
Spike your instincts
Engage

The meadows and prairies
Mountains and moors
Rivers and oceans
Pulse
While you flatline

Turn off Facebook
And turn on your heart
Engage from the basement of your being

You've trivialised life
with this byte-size-bullshit

Wake Up

Awaken
Awareness

Flex your solar plexus
Reconnect with your truth
There is a vortex of energy
waiting to be tapped
It swirls clockwise and anti

In anticipation
While you whistle
But when you stop and connect
to its source
that power will still and pool
into concentrated potion
Where passion aligns with purpose
and every question you ever asked
will be answered

Stall not
There is work to be done
and it's not the work
you've been doing.

A sickle moon hangs in the cleavage
of snow-capped mountains
It could be night or day
but time does not exist
in this magical place

Illusions are shattered
like yesterday's looking glass—
that reflection of former falsehoods

Voices follow thunder
Ancient spirits of the sky and sea
congregate like clouds
Eagle feathers and howling wolves
Drum beats and butterfly wings
Circling and warning
Hypnotic and stirring

The hidden truth
that sleeps and keeps
Perfectly preserved in the cross-hairs
of collective consciousness
until you remember
that kingdom at the edge of your senses, that

Indigo Portal
where an ocean stretches

A pristine sanctuary
where whales navigate by instinct
where peace radiates and ripples
where love echoes the loudest

Rise into your crown
Follow the stars between oceans
Your own celestial map
of impressionist pathways
that guide the lost away
from the sea of their own undoing.

A red moon
A howling wolf
Bloody earth and sky

We are born
Forged through many fires
And always turn to ash

These vessels that carry oxygen
and blood
are but a figment of importance

Like the sandalwood tree
Uprooted for its oil
We are sacred, yes
But permanent, no

We are not made of roots
You and I
Eternal seeds, we are
Magical beans / beings
Regenerating like cells

We will never be
And always be
The Jasmine Song of Whales

I am a

Mystic

descendent of the moon
before plates shifted
before mountains rose from ocean
when bones only told half the story
when lips carried messages
when secrets held wisdom,
not fear
a soul roaming between mother earth
and father sky
when the mind had wings, instead of bars
But
I am no sleeping giant
I hold this cosmos in my open palms
Maps, keys, treasure and blight
it spins
radiates
like a crystal ball in third dimension
Predestination is not straight
forward
and it is forward that we must follow

Spirit Message VI, 26 September 2016

Magic rain lights the sky
Sunlight glitters on an alpine trail
where winter's prisoners thaw
inside icy coffins

Shrapnel echoes through the woods
Pines are mystical soldiers
in a kingdom of lakes and boughs
that never break

Come now
Claws and beaks and baby feet
The voice of the wind is speaking
Mystery lives here
under bark and leaves
Journey with me through the trees
to the circle of sound
that spins round and round

Collapsible voices break
like twigs, when told to lie
The honesty of trees
get on your knees
Bees buzz low, below snow
put your ear to the ground
Hidden along ley lines, that zigzag like nerve endings,
Mother Earth is wired
to feed you what you need

Follow your path to reach your place, to forage your food
A mountain is there
your power is there
Track the ley to find your way
Cryptic we are
but not for long
Sing your song
the whale's song
it vibrates inside when you close your eyes
Close your eyes and go inside

Sweet child with so much love
release your heart
just start, just start
Follow me
toward the sea and sky, sand and trees
You're a nature Bee
Rare and buzzing with a low low hum
you're not a bird too close to the sun
Flight is interesting
take it from me
The sea, the sea, let's go to the sea
The tides, the moon that wax and wane
Follow their patterns
you'll shift, you'll stand
Your feet you'll find
you'll come alive
Alive, alive, you'll come alive
Trust me
Trust me

Part vi

*"Be love, and love will be
Be fear, and fear will be
You are what you are
always"*

Spirit Message VII, 30 September 2016

A bee hovers above my third eye
seeking pollen
in a lavender meadow
thickets, burst with fruit
The sky turns purple
the moon is full enough to suspend

horizons open at sunrise
New opportunity beckons
when you release yesterday's sunset
Allow the sun to be
to rise and set each day
move with this rhythm of renewal
and release
Love yourself
don't loathe or compare
The gift of love is yours to open and share

Hear the wind and birds calling you
closer to yourself
to the earth where your roots are buried
Feel them spread and stretch
like underground wings
that anchor and liberate
Be love, and love will be

Be fear, and fear will be
You are what you are, always
Forever changing
with infinite power to stay as long as you choose
So choose, make a choice to stay or move
Fear will find you if you harbour it
faith will set you free
yin and yang
instinct versus auto pilot

~

Open the door, let me in
Time is but a passing cloud
A passage of doorways,
entries and exits
blue lights and sultry nights
serenade and sway
colourful tongues that drip with sarcasm
why not, they say

Away, away, away for a day
our feet repeat
when words retreat
Vice advice
roll the dice
we are here, we are there
we are everywhere
inside, outside, the otherside, underside

Spirit Message VIII, 1 October 2016

A cloud looks at me
a star is near
Damascus[11] is calling

> *Don't wrinkle your face in confusion*
> *sometimes we journey through the night*
> *in the absence of light*

Damascus is not a place
It's a state of mind
a cinderella dream
a glass slipper made for you

You can't see your value
because your vision is impaired
with the gloom of your inner demons
They burn your flesh, cannibalise your soul
but still you let them
Why?
Why?

Ask yourself why
And then say
Enough
It's that easy if you decide
A circle is a circle, because it chooses to continue
A spiral[12] is something else

Seek to be a spiral, not a circle
You are loved, you are love
Why can't you see it?
Love love love love
Remind yourself
Love and acceptance
of self
This is how you will heal

Leda iii

Be-cone Or Become Extinct

There is a cave
tucked inside an Alpine mountain
A deep cave with a labyrinth of tunnels
A secret cave that no person could ever hope to find

In that cave lives a lonely dragon
who believes the stories of the one-dimensional world it inhabits
A dragon who is not allowed to be, or be seen, or be heard
for fear of being slain by a world that is wrapped up in its own prejudice and misconceptions
A dragon who has been hiding away its whole life
for fear of being feared

But, this dragon is slowly waking up
Its senses are stirring
Its innate knowing is being tapped
It is learning, day by day, that waiting on the world is to die, piecemeal

This dragon has yet to learn…
That its reservoir of fear
is easily eclipsed by its oceanic heart
That a dragon with more enemies than friends is destined for extinction

Don't let extinction be your fate, my dragon child

Enemies are simply people who are jealous, ignorant, or fearful of your power. You must not hide your power or you will die of impotence and not achieve your purpose.

The curlew's cry. Hear it wail. That is the sound of your spirit, begging you to save yourself from self-imposedchains and BEcome. You have a powerful mind, but you have trained it to work against you and bring obstacles. Life doesn't need to be a struggle, my love, so stop struggling and rise into your crown.

Leda iv

A Spider's Nature

From the mountain peak, I followed Leda deeper into the forest. On the way we passed mossy boulders and crossed a wooden suspension bri,dge. Tiny woodland birds flew in and out of the hollowed trunks of fallen gum trees, and black cockatoos screeched overhead. When we stopped, Leda pointed to an intricate and gigantic spider web that stretched between the branches of a hoop pine and a fig tree.

"Of all the creatures in the world, spiders are the most hated and feared. Would you agree?" said Leda.

"Yes," I said.

"Do you think that spiders are bothered by this fact?" she said.

"Probably not," I said, thinking about it.

"No," she said. "Spiders don't care what humans think of them, and they certainly don't try to change themselves in order to appease humans."

"That's a good point," I said. "I've never thought of it like that before."

"N should you. All your life, your parents, teachers, bosses, boyfriends, girlfriends, society...have tried to change your nature and dampen your spirits by criticising the very things that make you unique. And, while you have done a fine job at fighting back and staying true to yourself some of the time, you have also allowed those voices to infiltrate your internal chatter and undermine your instincts and confidence."

"I won't argue with that," I said. "I have been saying for years that I have an internal assassin inside me."

"You're not wrong," she said. "That internal assassin is real. It is an internal predator who has been forged from the fire of your own fear. From that constant voice of self-doubt that was nurtured by those naysayers who sometimes meant well and sometimes didn't. It may appear to be a sweet little cocker spaniel who has been around forever, but it is actually a wolf in sheep's clothing."

"Learning to disable my internal assassin is probably my greatest challenge of all," I said.

"You don't need to disable it," she said, "you just need to be aware of how it works and then train it to work with you instead of against you."

"How do I do that?" I said.

"Right now, in this moment, you can stop trying to change your nature. Just as we accept the spider for what she is, so too must you learn to truly accept and love yourself. The internal predator is strongest when you feed it."

"In other words, I've been feeding my predator from the deep well of self-loathing and I have the power to change its food source," I said.

Leda nodded.

The Forest

has burned
since my last visit
The leaves are flames
their stems ignited elements
where magic sparks
and life regenerates
mysteriously, but surely
Birth.
It arrives again.

~

The trees are tilted today
the mountain so blue
Some days
there are shades and hues
previously invisible

If days had moods
with soundtracks to accompany them
Today
I would be on my knees
with pianos and violins surging
and crashing
like waves on an isolated beach.

I found a

Unicorn
on its knees
in the forest
Its rainbow horn pulsed with magical power

It said...

*In your garden
is a tree with a radiant trunk
but it will only grow if you love yourself
unconditionally, every day*

*It's true that a rainbow needs
rain and sun
but not this one
This one only needs love
to stay luminescent
So love yourself, child, love yourself
Not for me, not for them
only for you
For you are as unique as a unicorn's horn
and magical in every way*

As will you
keep pushing through mud
keep reaching for sunshine

Love is the Lotus
that's attempting to bloom
THE ALMIGHTY STALK
adorned with mesmerising petals

On my desk
a dandelion trapped
inside a glass

Paperweight

I see myself
encased and sealed
a prisoner of my own making

A beautiful weed destined
to roam with trade winds
and explore the sky

A crystal ball with cryptic answers
A thousand tyrannised wishes
in a gypsy's palm

I free the paper from weight
and go in search of a hammer

The fairies signal me
with lights
Mirrored trees that flash
in rhythm with the falling sun
and rising moon

Snakes are ubiquitous
today
though scales are still
in hibernation

Millions of arbor bones
glow like phosphorous
when night seizes the sky

Spirits twist their nocturnal souls
into empty spaces
that beg to be filled

Upside down trees
and misty roads
lead me deeper into the forest
where a goddess calls me home

Fire and ash
Sage and feathers
Barefoot before
Naked still

I find the clearing
where Trees congregate
around the sacred one
Bark, the colour of ash
Leaves, the shape of fingerprints
And
when the wind blows around and through
its curvy branches
you can hear it speak
the Truth

She tells me to kneel
to open my palms for magic
to trade my world for hers
and I concur
for this skin can no longer
Breathe

Incognito

                    I wanted to be the boat
                       with its engine cut
              surrendering to an ocean of silence
                          so, I let myself

fall
overboard
like a scuba diver

                         Down
                         I sunk
               Hair billowing, like seaweed
                   A flotation of faith
                  that a message awaited

A passing

Sea Dragon

blew bubbles into my face
~ a magic spell
for underwater breathing

Though inter
dimensional currents
we travelled deep
beneath an ocean of sky
Our eyes shone like torches

         The sea dragon communicated, without speaking...

"Every step is important, nothing is wasted
Follow your heart, like you're following me
Trust your ability, like you're trusting me
Work hard, but don't lose sight of love and simplicity
Don't try to be something you're not
Simply be who you're supposed to be

You will become a beacon
when your learn to simply BE
when you learn to cut the engine
and tune out."

Leda v

The Spider and the Python

Leda told me to continue walking along the forest trail until I found a leopard tree with teardrops embedded in its trunk.

"Without you?" I said.

"I'll be back," she said and opened her wings. Like an arrow, she flew, head first. I watched her purple underbelly move between the spaces in the tree canopy, and then she was gone.

I followed the path into a dip, past caves and boulders, then up a steep slope where trees were thin and sunlight was dense. I stopped to smell the perfumed scent of the tiny orange, pink and yellow wild flowers that grew in clumps. That's when I spotted the leopard tree. I ran my fingers across the sandpapery bark; the teardrops were like the braille I had touched in a book. A spider, the colour of sunshine, parachuted down on a silk strand. Instinctually, I put my hand out to her and she climbed on.

"You have feared me your whole life," she said. "Why is today different?"

"I have been confronting my fears lately," I said, "and realising that they are unfounded."

"Good," she said. "I have been waiting to share my message with you for a long time. I have tried to share it on many occasions, but your fear always got in the way."

"I know," I said. "I'm sorry."

"Don't apologise for life lessons," she said. "They have all led you here to this moment in time. The time when you will be most receptive to receiving this particular lesson."

I nodded and smiled.

"In spiritual realms, Spider is guardian of the primordial

alphabet; the ultimate creator, and weaver of creativity. The reason she has visited you so many times, in dreams and physical form, is because you share her gift of creative weaving. When Spider visits you, she is trying to give you her spiritual medicine."

"Why has it taken me so long to reach this understanding?" I said, thinking about all the years I had viewed my spider dreams and encounters as negative.

"That is not important," she said. "You are here now, and now is all there is."

I nodded and smiled.

"In the human realm, Spiders are not community creatures (like most humans and animals). They are solitary."

"Another trait I can relate to," I said. "It seems that I have more in common with Spider than I thought."

"That is not all," she said. "Spiders also have an innate understanding and knowledge, deep within their core, that they possess everything they need to survive and thrive. They don't need to chase or hunt or prey. They simply find the best spot, spin their intricate webs, and wait for opportunity to arise. Spider's efforts and energy go one hundred percent into building her web. She is always prepared."

"Seems I have a lot to learn from Spider," I said.

"Yes, child, you do," she said. "Trust that you have everything you need to succeed, then prepare yourself for opportunity and strike when it arrives."

"Thank you for being patient with me, and thank you for the messages," I said.

"Call on me anytime," she said.

I watched her travel back up her silky ladder, and then sat at the base of the tree to think about what she'd said.

Minutes later, Python slithered down and around the

trunk. Her forked tongue danced with my scent.

"What have you come to teach me, old friend?" I said.

"I have come to remind you to shed your old skin," she said. "Old habits. Let them go. Accept that you are like me — you outgrow your old skin. Don't hang onto things and people who don't serve you. There is no guilt to be had for growth, transformation and evolution."

"I know this conceptually," I said, but humans essentially have layers of emotional and psychological skin to shed, and it's not always that obvious or easy to do. In a sense, you are forced to shed your old skin. It is nature's design."

"There are many different ways for a human to shed emotional and psychological skin. You learnt that at the start of your voyage with the medicine man."

"Yes, I forgot about that," I said.

"I am in the process of shedding my skin," she said.

"Take a piece for yourself and keep it in your pocket as a physical prompt to shed that psychological and emotional baggage that hinders you from growing and progressing. The fear that makes you live and love less than you deserve."

"Thank you, Python," I said, taking a piece of her skin.

"Call on me anytime," she said, and slithered back into the tree.

Part vii

"Your heart is your compass
just obey, don't betray
She'll show you the way
Okay?
Okay"

Spirit Message IX, 4 October 2016

She is a blue light moving in a figure of eight
Serpent-like

Duck your head, we're travelling
Follow the earth's skin
where darkness nourishes like the womb
The beginning, before the beginning
when self was aware, alive to the music within
the core of life, an apple's heart
de-seeded to make sense
of nonsense
no sense
Forgotten, forget not
forget-me-not
It's not a rhyme against time
the words of wisdom
they come from the source
the divine light that connects you

Open your heart
let it flutter like a butterfly
in flight
let it delight
Don't try and fight
go with the flow
these words are wise
except when you compromise

The old is cold, the new is bold
Unless you stay
Please don't stay
Be bold
Be bold
Semper Aurum Vedanta[13]

Gales and storms
ride not those waves that break your heart
Be true, be true, be you, be true
Truth is all that floats upon the ocean of time
Under the waves of yesterday
On the winds of chance
Take heed, I plead, listen to me

Let it go
That child who hurts
That child who hides her face from the sun because it burned so oft
Let her go, let her out
She's a sprite in the night with fairy's eyes
A world of joy she deserves to have
You cannot keep her locked up anymore
Be free
Be happy
Please
Smile and laugh
Show the world your heart
You precious child, you love, you light

Don't hide, don't hide
just say goodbye
The moon goddess glows for you
Rise into your crown of crystals
you jewel thief
with bag and torch
to incubate the sky

Feel those twinges
They are me
Reminder, reminding
Be kind to yourself

A ball of glass, of light
take flight
Become the ball, behold the light
Betwixt the sky, the perfect sky
Oh why do we try to pry
these lies from our heart
from the start
from the beginning
let's sing, let's curse, let's bring it all to our laps
Disgrace and love, and all that's out of sight
Kept hidden
for shame, for blame to keep
as tame
Be wild, I say
Be free like me
Behold this day, I will light the way, just say okay

Release, re-lease
Life anew
is what I give to you
So go, be free, liberate me
to see
to see
Underneath we go
to Glory go
for Glory is not in the sky
like a lullaby
She be low, down low
in the depths, she be free

Release, re-lease
Arrows of a compass
remember all four
stay grounded, be grounded
Your heart will always tell you where to go
listen not to anything else
your heart knows the way
just obey, don't betray
She'll show you the way
okay?
okay
Just say okay
Be love and be free
There is no-one like me

A Medicine Woman
lives inside me

The earth and sky call her
Mother

She,
the painted warrior
with eagle wings and celestial grace
is a frisson of power
Thunder in her eyes
and lightning in her hair

She calls me at night
when the moon is full
and the land is ready to purge

Leda vi

The Nile Crocodiles

I watched Leda shape shift from dragon to woman before she wrapped me in mottled python skin — a wise snake that shed its former self without hesitation, fear, or doubt. I pictured a decaying apple core preparing to return to the ground, from which it sprang, to feed worms in thanks and reciprocation for the food they once provided at birth. Like the snake who shed its skin and the tree who released ripe fruit, I was beginning to understand that I too would ultimately need to release outdated modes of behaviour and thinking before I could possibly hope to make room for something new.

I followed her into a labyrinth of caves, then deeper underground into a darkness so thick that I panicked and grabbed her hand. When she turned to face me, her green eyes shone like torch lights.

I read her mind and she read mine.

Do you trust me?

Yes.

I relaxed a little and let go of her hand. We travelled deeper and deeper down spiral stairs, carved of rock, until we reached the chasmic source. She kneeled down and crawled through a gap the height of a cobra in strike mode. I followed. Once inside the grotto we straightened our spines and stood upright. I walked toward the shimmering water and peered into it. My eyes glowed like sapphires, and the sound of trickling water echoed all around the cave.

"You can hear the water ghosts," said Leda.

"Water ghosts?" I repeated.

"The spirits of those who possessed the strength of

water in their earthbound lives," she said. "Spirits who saw themselves as sacred vessels holding water and learnt to trust the ebb and flow of the tides."

"That's poetic," I said.

"I'm in good company," she said and smiled.

She led me to the water's edge, where I had stood moments before. But this time, I saw a natural bridge made entirely of Nile crocodiles. Lined up, side by side, head to tail, tail to head - like stepping stones.

"The python skin you are wearing is to remind you that human transformation and evolution is only possible with growth and change. On the flip side, crocodiles have never had to change, adapt or evolve. They are still exactly the same creatures they were millions of years ago. This lesson is to teach you to call on crocodile when your life tests feel as threatening as the crocodile's death roll. Life tests that cannot be solved in the usual ways, but rather force you to trust your survival instincts and go deeper into yourself to find the answers."

"Okay," I said, wondering how this lesson would end.

"You have to travel this part of the journey on your own," said Leda, reading my mind again. "When you cross the crocodile bridge you will have two choices: to turn left or right."

"Which way do I go?" I said.

"Only you can decide," she said, "and there is no right or wrong way. There is always a choice between love and fear. Crocodile is a reminder to trust your instincts in the first instance, and, if all else fails, to go with the flow and trust the waters of life to lead you to your next lesson."

"Okay," I said, inhaling. I put my right foot onto the first crocodile's back, half expecting her to sink beneath, or react to, my weight, but she did not flinch. Instead, her scales began to vibrate. Feeling more relaxed, I took a second step so that my full weight was transferred to the crocodile. Vibrations traveled from my toes, up the length of my spine, swirling and collecting in my core, then moving gradually into my heart, my throat, my forehead, and finally my crown. Each step across the next crocodile activated these vibrations and each one transferred its energy into me. When I reached the other side of the water and stepped off the last crocodile, I looked back. Leda and the crocodiles had vanished and I was all alone.

I walked out of the cave and into an important decision. I had two choices. Left or right. My instinct told me to choose right, but the narrow path was dark and claustrophobic. I would have had to crawl through it like a miner in a shaft. I went left instead, where I could walk upright and see see light.

I wait for a butterfly's wing
to tap against my window with news
from the moon
Time traveller she is
with crucial messages

but all is quiet

I try to force a smile
and deny that my head has fallen
like a gum tree in the forest
thoughts spilt amongst moss and leaves
a rotting skull, with expired bones

A Woodland Death
befitting for a raven who believed it could shape shift

I live in a kingdom of clouds
this month
An April Fool
every damn day
Immobilised by demons that haunt me
still
like fingerprints I cannot alter
without fire, skinning, disfigurement

So weary and weak, this month
My sanity blindfolded and feet that shrink
instead of grow
Leaking more tears than these clouds
From friction and flux
Begging the moon to light the dark
While I'm incapable of sensing anything
Other than rain.

I am dying.

Like Summer at the hands of
Autumn

My wrinkles are really
fissures
on a skin fast tracked to shed

I consider fighting and resistance
but my energy is spineless
and my instincts know better

So I surrender, like a white flag
and trust this deconstruction
is the one I have contemplated
suicide for
The one who journeys alongside me
like a

Distant Memory

Death Should Come But Once

or twice
but I know Death
has blue eyes and violet cloak
He carries a monochrome cross
His hypnotic eyes scramble thoughts
His bottomless words alienate me
from my own voice, like a werewolf
on a moonless night

He hovers
like fog, close to the ground
Taunts and bludgeons
I look away
I look down
I look within, get lost
For those depths are deeper than the abyssal zone
Darker and colder
even for whales
who seek comfort in the midnight quarter

When death is near
lightning splits me in half
thunder crushes my bones
I renounce my faith in rainbows

Dig deep or die, he says
I only hover when you are on the verge of greatness or
darkness
and it is not your time to sleep

So take comfort in my eyes this day
the blue omniscience of being
at one with the dichotomy that usually divides
Not today, I say
Not today

Today, you will pick up your sword and decapitate all
that weighs you down
All that imprisons your mind, so mindlessly
Let it go and escape from the wilderness
That binds, blinds and gags you, child
Let it go and let Glory
The time for wallowing is past
The ghosts are nigh
Turn on the light, look beyond
your conditioning
There is sunshine in the sky
a rainbow too
If you look up, you will see it
It waits
It waits
But you must not wait anymore

Meet my depression
A crown of thorns
A monstrosity in my head
that renders my internal world as fragile
as a bee hummingbird in an ogre's hand
It makes the darkest corner more
cosy than a shooting star shower
It drowns all hope below the midnight sea

My admittance
is not an announcement of victimhood
It is progress
For it's taken twenty years to release
caged thoughts from captivity
to remodel an existential graveyard on Eden's garden
To learn

The Art of Surrender
much like the Sun
who cannot rise without a fall

I am nestled in the rainforest
just before the purge
the silence is too loud — even for me

While the storm postures
butterflies weave in and out of vines
clouds slide down the escarpment

A distant whistle
a nearby rustle
I'm trying hard
and not nearly hard enough
Perched

On The Verge

of an experience
that may never arrive

For now, though,
I belong to this moment
and this moment is where I belong.

Little birds
with rhinestone wings and shiny beaks
bring messages from afar
\hspace{4cm}the moon
\hspace{4cm}the desert
Someplace barren and arid
Mystical and mysterious

She sings from a star
Whispers my name
Summons my soul

But she is so far away
I can barely make out her words
Or is it me who's travelling away
I can never be sure
I seem so close to myself but far from her
And when we were close, I was not myself

Her presence hovers like a shaft of light
In a dark room
I am the smoke of incense
Wafting, curling, burning to a cinder
but it's not long before my mind
travels back to the

Burning Sun
that never sleeps

and always proves distracting

Still, to admonish myself now would be to deny that I have traversed a kingdom of wisdom

So I choose to ebb and flow
like the tide
Let the shells of lessons wash ashore
or sink beyond the sandbank

She waits for me, this much I know
Like the moon
who is full one day, invisible the next,
but always there
nonetheless

I am not myself
for the second winter in a row
But I have shed so much skin
already

So I let this miracle
Slither
at its own pace
Wrap its iridescent skin
around me

Because if this process has taught me anything
It is to trust the mystery of
Morphosis

Part viii

"Phoenix is made from ashes
Its strength forged through cremation
so it will never forget
its creation
its destruction
its genesis"

Spirit Message X, 2 December 2016

She taps on my ribs
It doesn't hurt
A warning to wake
To stay awake
Keep slumber at bay

Why did you leave me for so long?

I told you, Butterfly
When you're going through what kills
I am silent and still
Only you can travel when life threatens to unravel

Oh and what a sight for sore eyes
you are
who grows each day
like a mountain breaching the sea
A whale of a female you will be
It is destiny
Never forget
nor think it fairytale
for that is your earthbound self
whose wings were cut, torn, caged
set alight to burn as the
forests burn in their cleansing ritual
But phoenix is made of ashes
its strength forged through cremation
so it will never forget

its creation
its destruction
its genesis

You are my Phoenix
my only child
and I your mother
So sentimental I am toward you
my kin
my prospect, my star, my moon
Progression
You have progressed from prospect
to star, to moon
and you shine so brightly
To become a moon, one must break apart, bleed, purge,
regroup and rebuild
Only the strongest
achieve greatness
because they believed they could
They didn't accept what they saw with their eyes
but what they saw with their minds
in visions

Take your refuge in my arms
always and forever
I will smooth your passage
wherever you want to go
whatever you want
Tell me, don't ask
Tell me your desire, your need
and with magic I will grant it

You are ready to receive
my child
so open your hands, your arms
and receive
for there is only abundance in your heart
and destiny

The rabbit calls you
down its hole
Adventure awaits if you follow Queens
who don't wait to be offered a throne
Who take what is theirs
with confidence and grace
And you are full of grace
my child

The dragon
she is your guardian
She is me
in animal form
I am shape-shifter
Leda and I are one in the same
Leda
if you want a name for me child
call me Leda
for we are friends
as well as mother and daughter
and we will travel now as equals
between lessons
between lives
between kingdoms

She wraps me in purple silk
Mother moon kisses my forehead

Flowers grow wings
caterpillars walk upright

I want to vomit
purge the day
from my nighttime veins
The past rots inside me like
Leftovers

So I run naked into the woods
turn myself inside
out
Wait for the ravens
to get hungry

I decompose
in a meadow of wild honeybees
Violet-winged butterflies mate
below my ribs
A cicada hums six feet beneath my spine

In the brambles
my essence shifts into a Raven

Death is not so bad for a
Flower of the Earth

Leda vii

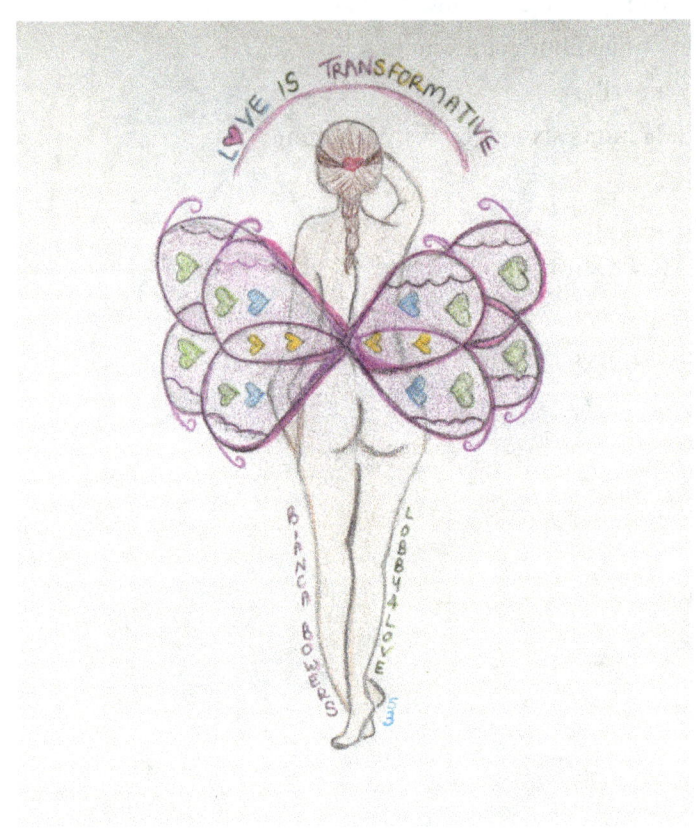

Ceremonial Wings

I woke at the edge of a lake surrounded by pine trees and thick with mist. The sun hung lower in the sky than usual, but it felt as cool as the moon. Beside me, Leda, the black dragon, with wings raised up over her head and obscuring her face.

"Leda," I said, touching her wing, "I have missed you so much."

She lowered her wings and turned to face me. Leda. Not in dragon form, but woman. Her dragon wings were still visible, but closed across her back, as if her shoulder blades were wings. She wore a ballgown made entirely of peacock[14] feathers, and her long, wavy, black hair framed her beautiful, petite face. Her green eyes and olive skin reminded me of the crocodiles in the grotto.

"After the crocodile bridge I turned left instead of right," I said. "I chose fear over love and lost myself in the wilderness all over again."

She smiled and said, "We are destined to repeat lessons, until we learn *the* lesson."

"Sometimes we journey through the night, in the absence of light," I said, quoting her own words.

"We wouldn't be here if you hadn't gone through the fire and risen from the ashes," she said.

I nodded.

She pointed to the centre of the lake, and said, "Your wings are ready."

I wasn't sure what she meant by wings, and I didn't have a chance to ponder or ask questions, because a dragon's head the size of a cathedral emerged from the black water of the lake.

I watched, speechless, as it rose upward until its entire body was revealed.

"A dragon-shaped castle," I said.

She stood up and took my hand. "Your wings are waiting inside."

We crossed a bridge that resembled a pier and was held in place by dragon claws. When we reached the castle door and crossed the threshold, the dragon bridge dissipated, much like the mist, leaving nothing but a reflection of the dragon castle in the black water.

The doors closed behind us and the castle submerged. In what seemed like a millisecond, Leda and I were back in the cave where I had lost my connection with her.

"You know what to do," she said.

"Yes," I nodded.

The right looked less daunting than it had done previously. I only had to crawl a few hundred metres before the dark tunnel opened up into an amethyst cave. Shafts of light refracted off the purple stones and created a dazzling effect. I explored the cave walls until I found a door. I took a deep breath before I entered.

Inside, the cave was dark and cool. A glass lantern sat atop a tripod. Inside the lantern, a violet and blue butterfly with flecks of silver in her wings. I didn't need to think. I knew the butterfly was me. My butterfly heart that I had trapped inside a glass lantern since I was a child and given to the dragon for safe-keeping. A butterfly who had grown to adulthood and was now fluttering in distress as it tried to break free. The tears began to flow when I realised what I had done. In my attempt to defend and protect I had merely trapped myself.

I dropped to my knees, lay on the floor, and sobbed. In

between sobs, I yawned. My mouth opened, as wide as a python's jaws, to release the river of pain that rushed and gushed like whitewater over jagged rocks. I released it all — like python shedding her entire skin — and emptied myself of all darkness and doubt, like a night sky transitioning into day. I lay there for hours. Empty of fear, and full of love. For myself, for my loved ones, for life, for Leda, for the voyage that had deconstructed and reconstructed me.

Then it was time to set her free. I held the lantern in my hands and she fluttered at the door to escape.

"I love you. I'm sorry. Please forgive me," I said, opening the tiny latch.

I placed my hand inside and she alighted on my palm. I walked her as far as I could — through the amethyst cave, along the dark tunnel, across the crocodile bridge, back up the spiral staircase, and outside to the lake. When she saw the light, her wings fluttered in anticipation and a new sensation of lightness and emancipation flooded my ribcage as she flew away.

I watched her flit, float, and fly across the lake, like a feather dancing in trade wind. When she disappeared into the pine forest, the mist had changed from thick clouds to thin smokey wisps and the scent of pines filled my nostrils. I leaned over the railing and peered into the black water of the lake to see two reflections. I looked up into the sky. There, on opposite sides, the sun and moon were visible. I smiled and thought about the significance for a moment.

"Balance," I said out loud. "I am closer to learning how to balance my dragon armour and vulnerable butterfly heart."

I go deep into the forest
to become a tree
The scent of pines comforts me

like the python skin in my pocket
neither are afraid of change
of burning to roots
of shedding scales

I have learnt this lesson too
to strike a match, to break skin
confront endings, welcome beginnings
lest I crash like timber
never wake from hibernation

When I emerge
the sky awaits me, like it always has
except I can reach it now

I yawn with the jaws
of a reticulated python
A cicada[15] is lodged
within the walls of my chest

Raven hears her urgent hums
and dives,
beak first, down my throat

when she emerges

The Cicada's Song

is on my lips

Take my hand
all ye woman who once were wild
and roam with me
through mountainous forests
until we find the lost girl
who smothered her spirit
in the tangled roots of belladonna

I no longer doubt

The Fates[16]

that blow me toward mountains
like an anabatic[17] wind

My resilient heart has healed
The passage of time
turned loss into gain

Feathers sprout
from cicatrices
Proof
that I had wings
all along

Spirit Message XI, 1 September 2018 at 9.05pm

A dragon silhouette flickers
above the raspberry candle
There is a spell upon my lips
Magic crackling, like a sparkler, in my heart

I have found the garden beneath my skin
Flowers of every hue in bloom
That magical forest she spoke of
was within me all along

Sunshine
like glitter on my face
I can see for the first time
Who I am
Who I was supposed to be all along

She is there
Always
A Velvet octopus reaching
the mountainous depths of me
The hidden sea

The room is silent while she speaks

My girl, my girl
I have missed you so
Smiling eyes when I see you now

Amidst magic stars and woodland trees
I give you my raven heart
with purple feather in its wing
And a dragon throne befitting of a queen
Stretch your wings, Butterfly
Blind you were, amnesia you had

Blindfolded by this veil of a life
But now you remember
You have been re-membered

A Phoenix rises
Gold glitter falls like rain from its feathers
It survived the sun's fire
the fire's flames
It was not born of ashes
It was the fire, shape
shifted its power
forged in a different way
from the same source
The source that birthed dragons
You are not a core element for nothing
You were not afraid of fire for nothing
Remember that
Remember why
These things you fear the most, are the things that made you

Rise, my Phoenix from the fire of your soul

Forge your own flight path to freedom
Sing
Sing
Sing
Your song
Sleep, no more, Butterfly
The journey continues whenever you call

Spirit Message XII, 12 September 2018 at 6.30pm

A sliver of moonlight
on the pine forest floor
A dragon is near
Her wings unfurling
Expanding
Preparing to fly
for the first time
She extends them like a cormorant with wet feathers
Flaps them back and forth
like a bush stone curlew

Doubt creeps along branches and pine cones
before it slithers to the ground
prepares to strike
at the moment she remembers herself
Her butterfly voyage
She levitates without thinking
Nothing can ground her
except herself

She breathes fire, doubt returns to dust

I watch her silhouette glide
past the butterfly moon
Hear a familiar voice behind me…

Those wings that look like ribs are real
and the pain is not mistaken
Butterfly

I will call you back when it's time
In time
It is time

~ The End ~

Butterfly Voyage Endnotes

1   Peyote is a cactus, and a Spanish word derived from "the Nahuatl, or Aztec, peyōtl, meaning "glisten" or "glistening". Other sources translate the Nahuatl word as "Divine Messenger".
SOURCE: https://en.wikipedia.org/wiki/Peyote

2   Ayahuasca is an entheogenic brew used as a traditional spiritual medicine in ceremonies among the indigenous peoples of the Amazon basin
SOURCE: https://en.wikipedia.org/wiki/Ayahuasca

3   The 7 Chakras: Sahasrara or crown chakra; Ajna or third-eye chakra; Vishuddha or throat chakra; Anahata or heart chakra; Manipura or solar plexus chakra; Svadhishthana or sacral chakra; Muladhara or root chakra

4   Jade is a "dream stone" and assists in recognising yourself as a spiritual being on a human journey. (The Crystal Bible, Judy Hall, page 152)

5   "Bats with batons" is a reference to authority and those who blindly do what they're told

6   "Wimps and beards" is a reference to old white men, especially in Biblical times when men of the cloth were kings.

7   "Dope and hogwash" refers to religious guilt and brainwashing.

8   "Chosen kingdom" is a reference to the Matriarchy

9   "When she remembers" is a reference to women and the rebirth of matriarchy and feminine power.

10   In biblical terms Galilee is where Jesus performed many miracles: Walked on Water, Fed the Five Thousand, and Turned Water Into Wine. It is also where the resurrection took

place.

Geographically, Galilee is a mountainous region in Northern Israel with low temperatures and high rainfall. Flora and Fauna thrive and many birds migrate from colder climates.

    SOURCE MATERIAL:-

    https://en.m.wikipedia.org/wiki/Galilee

In addition, when researching this reference I came across an account written by an archaelogist in Galilee who commented on the amount of cicadas there were during Summer. This is significant because of the references to: "cicadas", "the cicadas song", and "You songbird of galilee".

11   Damascus is one of the oldest inhabited cities (as early as 8000 to 10,000 BCE). It became a base for the Byzantine Empire, and it is surrounded by an oasis. Today, it is the capital of the Syrian Arab Republic and is colloquially known as the "City of Jasmine". Damascus experiences a semi-arid climate because of the rain shadow effect (a phenomenon of dryness that is caused by the mountains that block the passage of rain-producing weather systems).

SOURCES:-

https://en.m.wikipedia.org/wiki/Damascus

https://en.m.wikipedia.org/wiki/Rain_Shadow.

12   The sacred spiral is an ancient symbol of spirituality, specifically as a symbol of ascension. The Celts, for example, believed it represented movement through life experiences.

SOURCE:-

goldenageofgaia.com/20111/08/16/the-sacred-spiral

There is also a reference to a 'spiral' in the first Spirit Message.

13   "SEMPER AURUM VEDANTA" - This is a reference that I had to do extensive research in order to understand the meaning.

I had heard the word 'Semper' before, but the words 'Aurum' and 'Vedanta' were unfamiliar. After some research, I have come to translate the phrase as 'Knowledge is always gold', but I suspect that there is much more to it. Vedanta is one of the six orthodox schools of Hindu Philosophy, and the word literally means 'the end of the vedas'.
SOURCE: https://en.m.wikipedia.org/wiki/Vedanta

14   In Egypt, the Peacock is associated with the Sun god, Ra. It is also the closest description to the mythical Phoenix. As a spirit animal guide, the peacock helps us shed old feathers of the past and reclaim the true beauty of our individuality.
SOURCE: www.shamanicjourney.com/peacock-power

15   As a spirit animal guide, the Cicada symbolises what we were (nymph) and all the glory of what we've
become (adult). Unlike the moth and butterfly that
undergo complete metamorphosis, cicadas have no pupal state. Interestingly, the follow up to *Butterfly Voyage*
(should I write it) is titled *The Cicada's Song*.
SOURCES:
https://en.m.wikipedia.org/wiki/Cicada
https://www.cicadamania.com/cicadas/what-do-cicadas-symbolize/

16   The Fates - Greek & Roman mythology for Fate/destiny

17   Anabatic wind- from Greek 'anabatos', meaning moving upward. A warm wind which blows up a slope, driven by heating of the slope through isolation.
SOURCE:
https://en.wikipedia.org/wiki/Anabatic_wind

Acknowledgements

Many thanks to the following:-

THE EDITOR OF SHOT GLASS JOURNAL ISSUE #15 FOR PUBLISHING THE FOLLOWING POEMS:
- Distant Memory
- Morphosis
- The Fates

PATREON-TRIAL SUPPORTERS:
- Caryl Bosman
- Neil Young
- Steve Porter
- Mark Gladman

About the Author

Bianca Bowers is a South African-born, Australian-based writer who has also lived in the UK and New Zealand. She holds a BA in English and Film/TV/Media Studies and her poetry has appeared in film, online journals and print anthologies over the last twenty years.

Bianca has authored five poetry books and one novel. Her second novel, *Three Hearts,* is due in 2020. When Bianca isn't writing, she is most likely exploring the Mt Coot-tha running trails with her rescue hound, Honey.

You can find Bianca at:
www.biancabowers.com

To leave a review, please visit:
https://amazon.com/author/biancabowers
https://www.goodreads.com/BiancaBowersAuthor

www.ingramcontent.com/pod-product-compliance
Lightning Source LLC
Chambersburg PA
CBHW051945290426
44110CB00015B/2116